BOLD KIDS

CHILDREN'S MOUSE & RODENT BOOK

No part of this book may be reproduced or used in any way or form or by any means whether electronic or mechanical, this means that you cannot record or photocopy any material ideas or tips that are provided in this book.
Copyright 2022

All images in this book have been reproduced with the knowledge and prior consent of the artists concerned, and no responsibility is accepted by producer, publisher, or printer for any infringement of copyright or otherwise, arising from the contents of this publication.

If you are looking for fun facts about hamsters, read on. This adorable little mammal is a popular pet choice and can teach kids how to take care of a pet.

These fun facts will make learning about the hamster an interesting experience for both you and your kids. Find out why they are so popular and learn a few interesting facts about them, too. Let's get started.

What is the life span of a hamster? The average hamster lives between two and three years. Some species, such as Russian chamsters, can live even longer. This article will provide kids with some fun facts about hamsters.

The following information is provided as a guideline for educating the younger generation about this adorable animal. For example, the average sexoriented hamster can live for about eight years.

Why are hamsters a good pet for children? First of all, they are small and fun to play with. You can easily keep a hamster in your home and keep it happy by providing a fun environment for your children to play with.

They are also friendly towards other animals and will not bite or spit out on your kids if they accidentally bump into them. And if you're worried about your hamster being aggressive, you can get one of them as a pet.

The hamster is a unique animal that is adapted to living in an urban environment. The most common variety of hamster is the Chinese hamster. These creatures are nocturnal, and most live in deserts.

They have great eyesight and are capable of navigating by using their senses. A black-bellied pig is one of the most extreme examples of a hamster and is a great choice for kids!

Apart from having a unique appearance, a hamster has a very short lifespan compared to other critters. They have a lifespan of two to three years in captivity, but in the wild, a hamster can live up to six years.

They are very energetic animals, and are great pets for children. If you have a hamster at home, he'll surely love your pets.

A hamster is one of the smallest pets in the world. However, despite its small size, a hamster can be a very fun and fascinating pet for kids.

Whether you're considering a homing hamster for your family, a hamster is a great pet for kids. If you are not sure about homing a rat, you can get a hamster that mimics your human.

While hamsters can be fun pets for kids, they can also be dangerous. They are known to catch colds from humans, so it's a good idea to keep them away from them and out of reach of children.

You can find a hamster in your neighborhood by asking a friend or relative for a hamster. In addition to a hamster's short lifespan, it's a fun and interesting pet for kids.

Did you know that hamsters can live up to eight years? That's a pretty impressive lifespan for a small animal. While hamsters are small and cute, they can also be quite destructive.

While the hamster's tiny size is a great trait for a pet, it is essential to remember that a rogue a hamster can't live in a cold or windy environment.

Did you know that hamsters are naturally nocturnal? They have short legs, a short tail, and small ears. They're also very territorial.

This means hamsters aren't the best pets for children, but they're still fun to play with. If you're looking for a hamster for your kid, here are some fun facts about hamsters for kids.

Apart from their tiny size, hamsters are also incredibly intelligent. They can run for as long as five and a half miles a night.

They're very fast – they can move from one place to another in just a few seconds. A few interesting facts about hamsters can help you decide if a tame hamster is a good fit for your child.

Lightning Source UK Ltd.
Milton Keynes UK
UKHW051916100922
408607UK00005B/135